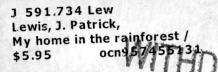

my home in the rainforest

J. Patrick Lewis

Children's Press®
An Imprint of Scholastic Inc.

Library of Congress Cataloging-in-Publication Data

Names: Lewis, J. Patrick, author.
Title: My home in the rainforest/by J. Patrick Lewis.
Description: New York: Children's Press, an imprint of Scholastic Inc.,
2017. | Series: Rookie poetry animal homes | Includes index.
Identifiers: LCCN 2016030840| ISBN 9780531228739 (library binding) | ISBN
9780531230084 (pbk.)
Subjects: LCSH: Rain forest animals—Juvenile literature.
Classification: LCC QL112 .L493 2017 | DDC 591.734—dc23
LC record available at https://lccn.loc.gov/2016030840

Produced by Spooky Cheetah Press
Design by Judith Christ-Lafond

© 2017 by Scholastic Inc.

Printed in China 62

SCHOLASTIC, CHILDREN'S PRESS, ROOKIE POETRY™, and associated logos are
trademarks and/or registered trademarks of Scholastic Inc.

1 2 3 4 5 6 7 8 9 10 R 26 25 24 23 22 21 20 19 18 17

table of contents

welcome to the
rainforest

Over half the world's creatures call it home
in a kingdom where wonders are found.
It is the "jewel of the Earth." Its thick trees
may keep sunlight from reaching the ground.

Rainforests contain evergreen trees. Their leaves never fall off.

gorilla

Who is the burliest brute in the jungle?
Who can scare you with just one stare
or a couple of thumps on the barrel
of his silverback chest. Beware!

Adult gorillas can eat up to 66 pounds of plants and fruit in a day.

jaguar

A cat can move with **stealth** and speed
when hunting **prey** on which to feed.
But let her be a warning sign:
Sadly, the jaguar is in decline.

Mother jaguars live with their cubs. Most of the time, adult jaguars live alone.

boa constrictor

This snake is the stuff of nightmares.
Females are bigger than males.
You are likely to see them hanging around
in rainforest trees and on trails.

Boa constrictors do not chew their food. They swallow their prey whole.

red-tailed monkey

A monkey gets ready to jump,
but he says, "Why am I such a grump?
Oh, go hang! Give me strength.
I should welcome the length
of the handle I have on my rump!"

Red-tailed
monkeys
use up to 22 sounds
to communicate.

toucan

I am mainly a fruit-eating bird,
who gives the whole jungle a thrill
by wearing this slightly absurd,
fantastic banana-shaped **bill**!

Toucans make their nests in tree holes. They do not lay down sticks, straw, or any other nesting materials.

amazonian centipede

Once a centipede said on vacation,
"Do not bug me—I'm into **gyration**.
When I go on my trips, I'm so hip that my hips
hula one hundred times in rotation."

A lot of people think amazonian centipedes have 100 legs. They do not! These creepy crawlers have 42 or 46 legs.

jungle homes

Let the rainforest be our house of hope
under a canopy of trees.
Where else can you see a **biosphere**
in infinite varieties?

All the animals shown in this book are hiding in this photo. Can you find them all?

fact files

	Gorilla	Jaguar	Boa Constrictor
HOW BIG AM I?	up to 6 feet 3 inches tall (taller than many adults)	up to 9 feet long, including the tail (longer than a motorcycle)	13 feet long (almost as long as a small car)
HOW MUCH DO I WEIGH?	up to 430 pounds (more than an upright piano)	up to 250 pounds (about 3 German shepherd dogs)	60 pounds (more than an 8-year-old child)
WHAT DO I EAT?	fruit, leaves, stems, seeds	fish, turtles, deer, capybaras, tapirs	birds, monkeys, wild pigs